Cadence of the Unsaid

Musings of the Soul

Anurag Tamoli

BookLeaf Publishing

India | USA | UK

*To my beloved Dehradun, the majestic mountains,
and to all who find solace in the beauty of
literature, and to the voices that stand resilient
amidst chaos.*

Acknowledgement

This book would not have come into existence without the love, guidance, and inspiration I have been fortunate to receive from so many remarkable people in my life.

I extend my heartfelt gratitude to my parents, whose unwavering love and support have been my greatest strength. Your belief in my dreams has inspired me to pursue this creative journey. To my friends, thank you for your companionship, laughter, and encouragement—your presence has made every moment meaningful.

I am deeply thankful to my teachers, whose guidance and passion for literature have shaped my writing and deepened my love for words. To the writers who have inspired me, your works have opened my mind and helped me discover my voice.

A special acknowledgment goes to Dehradun, whose beauty and tranquility have provided a rich backdrop for my reflections and creativity. Finally, to the world of literature, thank you for being my sanctuary. This book is a testament to all of you who have nurtured my spirit and inspired me to express the unsaid.

Preface

This book is born from a fragment of my heart, steadfast in its belief in voicing the unspoken and raising an outcry for all that demands to be heard. Each poem stands as an intimate expression of the quiet resilience found in nature, the beauty of silence, and the simple, often overlooked moments that fill life with meaning. Through this collection, I strive to give words to experiences that transcend language, capturing the essence of both personal and universal truths.

The verses within reflect the one-on-one encounters with life's subtleties—the whispering valleys, the gentle knock of winter, the fading light of lazy evenings, and the solace found in quiet corners. Here, nature is more than a setting; it is a companion offering solace and strength, inviting readers to pause, breathe, and reconnect with themselves.

Yet, these poems are also a call to consciousness. They speak to the political struggles of our time, reminding us of humanity's capacity to endure and rise above adversity. In these turbulent times, this collection doesn't shy away from the complexity of social and political unrest. Instead, it seeks to portray humanity's courage and resilience in the face of challenges.

May this collection inspire reflection, encourage hope, and remind readers of the enduring beauty and strength that lies within us all.

Winter's Gentle Knock

One morning, winter knocked on the window
of my heart
 draped in an angelic white robe and a crown
of ice twinkling in her hair
 and woke me from the autumn slumber of
fading warmth,
 whispering tales of frosted dawns and
silver-laced dreams,
 her breath a cold caress upon my soul,
promising stillness
 and the quiet elegance of a world wrapped in
snow.

She took me into her world, held my hand so tenderly,
 leading me through a landscape of silenced whispers,
 where every snowflake danced like a frozen tear,
 and the sky wore a veil of pale blue light.
 With each step, her touch melted the remnants of autumn's hue,
 and in her embrace, I found the solace of stillness,
 a quiet lullaby beneath the snow-laden trees.

Away from the mortal's plain, she dwells in the mountain's solace,
 in the midst of the fog, she dances like a goddess, serene and untamed.
 She spreads her milky veil, under which the tired earth rests,
 cradled in her motherly arms, lulled into a tranquil slumber.

With gentle grace, she prepares the earth for
spring's awakening,
 calming its restless spirit, softening the soil
with her touch,
 till all is quiet, waiting, beneath her watchful
gaze.

She and I, bound by the whispers of the cold
wind,
 shared a quiet language, unspoken yet true.
 In her frosted touch, I found my reflection,
 a soul awakened, inspired, renewed.
 As the snowflakes kissed the earth in her
tender embrace,
 I felt her presence linger in my heart's quiet
place,
And though seasons may change and time
may depart,
 she'll always be the winter that stirs the fire
in my heart.

Whispers of the Valley

How can we sleep when the whispers fade,
Of ancient trees in the twilight shade?
Their limbs outstretched in a silent plea,
Roots entwined with the earth, yearning to
be free.

In their being resides the history of ages,
The sweet and sour memories of days gone
by,
Echoes of life etched in their pages,
As seasons turn and years drift by.

The valley's beauty breathes through their
veins,
They stand like sentinels through sun and
rain.
As much a part of this land as we,
They hold its soul, its memory.

Oh, dwellers of this sacred ground,
Recall the past where echoes resound.
Remember Gaura Devi, who clasped the
trees,
In defiance bold, with whispered pleas.

With fearless grace, she wrapped her arms,
Around the forest, warding off harms.
Unbowed by threats, her spirit aflame,
She shielded the woods from the hands of
shame.

She faced the greed of those who'd claim,
This land for profit, without remorse or
name.
But her heart, like a mountain, unbroken and
wide,
Kept the green sanctuary safe on her side.

So how can we sleep while her spirit calls,
Through the rustling leaves and waterfalls?
The trees are her legacy, living and grand,
Let us stand with her, hand in hand.

Lazy Evenings in the Hills

Lazy evenings in the hills,
laden with the scent of pine and tranquility.
Far far from the madding crowd,
Lost in unheard melodies.

Every evening with a flavor of its own
and every sunset with its shade.
Where breeze fills the heart
with pleasant memories of the good past and
some aches.

When Daisies turn yellow
and pages of the book begin to flitter
and the loafing golden bends shine.
Steadily the charming moon appears on the
darkening sky
and so begins the wait of the poet and the lover.

Somewhere Far in the Hills

Somewhere far in the hills,
by the hearth, one sits, wandering down
memory's lane.
Where the scent of cinnamon and pine
once intertwined with moments past's refrain.

Outside, the window paints the evening red,
unearthing buried lore,
Reviving forgotten whispers,
the sky brushed with nostalgia's score.

The wind's soft dance summons
bliss lost in times gone by,
While the snow's gentle touch rekindles tales,
 And sparks memories to fly.

Amidst Earth's snowy shroud,
a resilient flower takes its role,
Its petals unfurling,
Promising spring's eternal soulful stroll.

The Mountain's Secret

Mountains stand, both still and new,
Silent giants beneath skies so blue.
Though rooted firm, they rise and bend,
Each curve a path, each turn a friend.

Unmoved they seem, yet ever change,
With every step, a fresh, strange range.
Beauty waits in mist and hue;
Life, like mountains, is shifting too.

We climb the heights, we breathe the air,
Finding hidden wonder there.
Stable, strong, yet always free,
Mountains are what life aspires to be.

For life is thrilling, bold as the peaks,
Where courage climbs, and wonder speaks.
In the heights of hope, in valleys below,
Life, like mountains, is where beauty grows.

Petals of Serenity

I am the blossom in the wild, serene,
Pure and bright, with a gentle sheen.
Untouched by the world's deceitful art,
A symbol of grace, with the purest heart.

Soft as the snow on the mountain's crest,
In my solitude, I find my rest.
A tranquil spirit, peaceful and still,
With the music of life, my veins fill.

I drink from the dew of untouched air,
Caressed by the winds, light and fair.
Far from the clamor, from worldly guise,
I bloom where silence embraces the skies.

Cradled in moonlight, bathed in stars,
I glow unseen by the city's scars.
Rooted in wisdom, ancient and deep,
Where the echoes of the earth softly sweep.

I am Brahmakamal, rare and true,
Blooming where only the purest winds blew.
In the wilderness, my beauty grows free,
A testament to all that life can be.

I stand as a symbol of hope's quiet might,
Holding my ground through the long, cold night.
With each gentle petal, I breathe and I sing,
The promise of dawn and the joy it will bring.

A Pause in the Wilderness

There are days when the weight is too much
to bear,
When the world feels heavy and life's unfair.
It's okay to wander, to seek an escape,
To rest from the rush and let worries
reshape.

For life can be tiring, wearing us thin,
Needing time and space to renew from
within.
To breathe and to pause, to find one's way,
To gather strength for another day.

In the arms of nature, solace is found,
Where the heart beats calm and the soul is
unbound.
Where rivers sing softly and trees stand tall,
Nature's embrace can heal it all.

So take that step, retreat for a while,
Find peace in the green, let go and smile.
For to rest is to mend, to feel whole once
more,
And return to life stronger than before.

Where Love Blooms

Somewhere under the sky,
Between the snow-clad mountains,
Under the great cherry blossom tree, we lay—
Wrapped in each other's warmth,
As our love mingles so softly.

Far, far away from
Every fear, judgment, bondage, and hate,
Where you flow in my tears
And I run in your veins.

Where our hearts beat as one,
And love penetrates our souls,
Where all I am is you,
And you are me.

In that sacred space,
We will be one forevermore.

In the Shadows of May

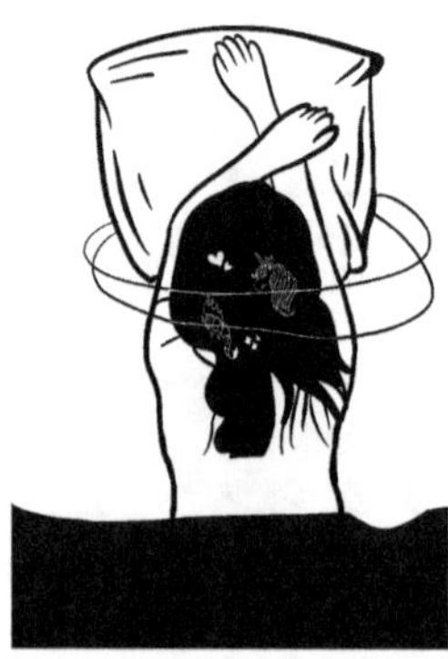

A closed door and tears cascading down,
That was the burden weighing on my heart
during the month of May.
Once, I was the life of every gathering,
A beacon of laughter, brightening the darkest
days.
But now, I find myself a mere shadow,
A low-spirited figure seated in the corner of
an empty ground,
Lost amidst the echoes of joy that once
enveloped me.

This is the insidious grasp of a devil named
Depression,
It stealthily snatched away the light from my
life,
One by one, my cherished ones drifted away,
Leaving behind an echoing silence that
screams of their absence.

Waking up feels like embarking on a
relentless battle,
Each day, a war against the heaviness that
clings to my soul.
Nightfall becomes my sanctuary,
When the world and its relentless shams fade
into oblivion.
In the stillness of darkness, I find solace,
Yet the shadows of my thoughts gnaw at my
peace.

Slowly, oh so slowly, this feeling consumed
me,
An invisible thief, stealing my will to fight,
It swept through my mind like a dark tide,
Neither the world outside nor you noticed
the tempest within,
As I spiraled deeper into a solitude that felt
unending.

Motivational quotes, well-meaning words of
encouragement,
All fell flat, echoing hollowly against the walls
of my despair.
Like a haunting refrain, my dreams morphed
into cries for help,
Drowned beneath the weight of unfulfilled
aspirations,
Once vibrant, now faded, like distant stars
losing their glow.

Yet in this darkness, a flicker of resilience
stirs,
A whisper of hope that dares to challenge the
shadows.

Though the road ahead seems fraught with
uncertainty,
I hold onto the fragile thread of tomorrow,
Yearning for the dawn to break through the
gloom,
And perhaps, to find my way back to the
light,
To reclaim the laughter, the joy, and the love
That once danced so freely in my heart.

Moonlit Solace

One night, I slipped from my room,
chaos stirring inside, a storm unbridled—
and I found myself on an empty road,
my heart thundering as if bound for war.

But then, a friend came to my side,
the gentle wind, noticing my plight,
and in a soft embrace, she held my cheeks,
her cool fingers flushing them with life.

With a touch like woven silk,
she lifted my chin, tenderly guiding my gaze,
unveiling the radiant moon, once hidden
behind veils of wandering clouds.

The moon, unveiled and bright,
became my silent, steadfast companion—
its silver gaze casting gentle light
over my lonely, hurried steps.

And so we walked, the moon and I,
my burdens eased by her quiet glow,
each step a little softer, lighter,
as if her light was lifting me whole.

Haven of Four Walls

After days that stretch and strain,
through the clamor, through the ache,
there's only one place I yearn to be—
the quiet warmth of my own space.

My room, a small and hidden world,
its four walls more than bricks and stone;
each corner cradles bits of me—
my own reflection, etched and grown.

It's where my weary soul unwinds,
where secrets softly slip and spill,
a sanctuary shaped by dreams,
my little universe, hushed and still.

This isn't just four walls and floor,
it breathes, it holds, it knows me well—
it's a living part of who I am,
a tender story, a sheltering shell.

And when the world grows far too loud,
I find peace beneath its gentle light,
within this room, this heart of mine—
I lay down my burdens and rest at night.

The Priceless Hours

In a world that rushes past, so fast,
we forget what matters most—
these moments shared, rich and rare,
with those who feel like home.

A simple cup of chai or coffee,
conversation soft and slow,
where laughter fills the air like song,
and silences feel whole.

No treasures glinting gold or bright
could buy the bliss we find—
a space to share, to laugh, to cry,
to ease a troubled mind.

It's here we grow, we learn to be,
held firm by shoulders strong,
a place to rest when the road is rough,
where we feel we belong.

What a privilege, to call this ours,
these hours, this warmth, this light—
to gather close with friends, with kin,
our anchors through the night.

For in their eyes, we see ourselves,
and in their hearts, we know,
that love and time, bound hand in hand,
are gifts that let us grow.

Forgotten Corners of a City

The Doon I knew fades quietly,
its once-green heart now steel and stone;
where litchi trees lined the roadsides,
their shadows cool, their branches grown,
there's only pavement, bare and cold—
a bustling town where silence strolled.

Gone are the sleepy bookshops,
their musty pages filled with lore,
and cinema halls that stood so grand
now whispers of a time before.
Corners lost to concrete towers,
to glass and glare and numbered hours.

In place of cafés, quiet, small,
where laughter once mixed with the air,
there rise the walls of sleek facades,
leaving no trace that we were there.
Each space a shadow, faintly drawn,
etched in hearts long after gone.

The trees that canopied these streets,
that shaded steps and softened sound,
now felled or lost in tarmac's sprawl—
no cover left, no rooted ground.
A city changed, grown loud and fast,
its gentle rhythm left in the past.

And those canals that carved their way
like veins that ran through Doon's still heart,
now buried, closed, as rivers slept,
tamed by roads that pull apart
the quiet paths where water sang—
a melody now long un-sprung.

But memory keeps those streets alive,
where laughter mingled with the breeze,
where books and films and idle chats
once filled the city's gentle ease.
The Doon we knew, that small town grace,
lost in time, a sacred place.

The Art of Slowing Down

In the sound of silence, morning breaks,
gentle whispers as the world awakes.
The light spills softly through the pane,
each beam a promise, free from strain.
A moment to breathe, to simply be,
in the hush of dawn, there's clarity.

A shared quiet, two souls intertwined,
in a café nook, with thoughts aligned—
the silence wraps us like a warm embrace,
each glance tells a story, no need for haste.
We sip our coffee, let time unwind,
in these small stillnesses, true peace we find.

In the evening's calm, when the world slows
down,
the night brings solace, a velvet gown.
Stars blink softly, secrets shared in the dark,
each flicker a reminder, a subtle spark.
In the quiet of night, we find our rest,
the beauty of stillness, a gentle caress.

Joy blooms in doing the small, simple
things—
a book in hand, the joy that it brings,
the rustle of pages, the worlds we explore,
or a leisurely walk, where worries are no
more.
Sitting in sunbeams on winter's soft ground,
gardening dreams where peace can be found.

Reconnect with hobbies long left behind,
let creativity flow, let your spirit unwind.
A paintbrush, a pen, the clay in your hands—
in these little moments, life gently expands.
Spend time with yourself, let thoughts freely
roam,
in solitude's embrace, you'll discover your
home.

Engage with the echoes of memories past,
the laughter, the tears, the friendships that
last.
In revisiting times that shaped who we are,
we find joy in journeys, like a guiding star.
And when loved ones gather, hearts open
wide,
in their laughter and warmth, we truly abide.

So let us slow down, breathe deep, and
embrace
the richness of life at a tender pace.
For in every silence, in each gentle sigh,
we find the beauty of living—our spirits fly.

Echoes of the Helpless Heart

Each dawn breaks, and here I am again—
falling for you, lost, without end.
I try to escape, to turn away,
yet with every breath, you choose to stay.

Your scent fills my heart, my soul, my mind,
in every whisper, your presence I find.
My body chills at your memory's touch,
a quiet ache that's almost too much.

My heart races like a train in flight,
lips tremble, eyes blurred with light.

Butterflies stir, restless, alive,
each thought of you a honeyed knife.

I think of the day I first saw you near,
your beauty like moonlight, piercing and
clear—
you were the moon to my darkest night,
a quiet glow, serene and bright.

Oh! I try so hard to break these chains,
to silence the storm that calls your name,
but helplessly, day after day, I fall—
forever yours, beyond my control.

Veils of Forbidden Love

In shadows deep, where our secrets lie,
two hearts collide, yet must deny.
A glance, a touch—a fleeting spark,
in a world of light, we love in the dark.

Your laughter dances through the air,
like whispered dreams, we find our flare.
But love, it seems, has drawn the line,
forbidden paths, a bond divine.

We meet in places not our own,
where silence shields the love we've sown.
Each stolen moment, a fleeting thrill,
in quiet corners, we breathe, we fill.

Yet every heartbeat bears the price,
the weight of longing, the roll of dice.
For every kiss beneath the stars,
carries the burden of hidden scars.

In an intolerant world, where norms stand
tall,
where love is met with shadows and walls.
Violence brews where acceptance should be,
bloodshed and fear stifling hearts that long to
be free.

The fear of separation grips us tight,
as society's judgment looms like a blight.
Yet amidst chaos, we seek our grace,
finding solace in a forbidden embrace.

The world outside may never see,
the beauty wrapped in secrecy.
For love that blooms in shadows cast,
is like a dream, too bright, too fast.

So here we stand on edges thin,
with aching hearts, we wear our sin.
For in this dance of wrong and right,
forbidden love ignites the night.

Though storms may rage and time may part,
you'll always dwell within my heart.
In whispers soft, our souls will meet,
a love that's true, though bittersweet.

First Steps into the Unknown

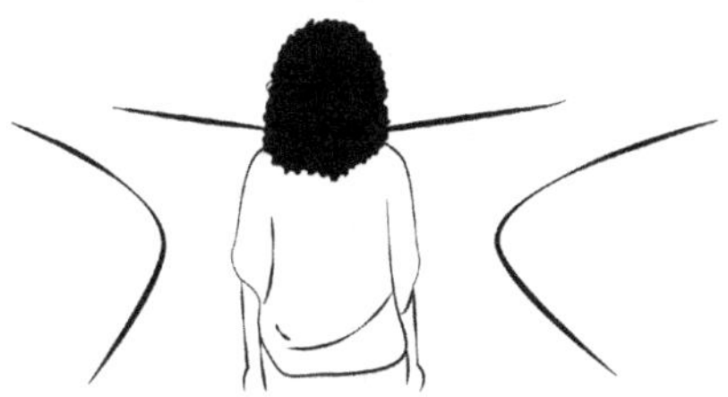

With trembling hands, I close the door,
leaving behind the life I adored.
Each creak of the floor, a whisper of pain,
echoes of memories like a soft, gentle rain.

The world outside feels vast and strange,
a canvas unwritten, ready for change.
Anxiety wraps me in its tight embrace,
as I step into the shadows of this unfamiliar
space.

New hopes bloom like flowers in spring,
promises of laughter and joy they bring.
I dream of a future where I stand tall,

where I make myself proud, and answer the
call.

Yet fear clings close, a ghost in my mind,
what lies ahead, I'm scared to find.
The bustling streets, they pulse with life,
but I feel the weight of the silent strife.

Each corner I turn holds a reminder of
home,
the warmth of my mother, the comfort I'd
known.
Homesickness wraps me in a blanket of
grief,
as I navigate through the longing for relief.

But deep within, a flicker ignites,
a spark of courage to embrace new sights.
For in every tear lies a story untold,
a journey of strength, a heart brave and bold.

I breathe in the air, thick with the new,
the taste of adventure, the thrill of the true.
With every step, I loosen the past's chain,

in this city of dreams, I'll dance through the
pain.

Though the road may be winding, uncertain,
and long,
I'll weave my own path, I'll learn to be
strong.
For in every goodbye, there's a promise to
grow,
toward a life filled with love, as bright as its
glow.

Angels in Disguise

In the tapestry of life, woven tight,
you emerged like a star, brilliant and bright.
Through shadows and storms, you stayed by
my side,
a beacon of hope, my unwavering guide.

With gentle hands, you held my own,
through trials and fears, I was never alone.
In moments of doubt, when the path seemed
unclear,
your voice whispered softly, "I'm right here."

You showed me the way when I stumbled and
fell,

your faith in my dreams, like a magical spell.
With patience and wisdom, you opened my
eyes,
revealing the strength hidden deep in my
sighs.

Through thick and through thin, you stood
steadfast,
a mentor, a friend, our bond unsurpassed.
In laughter and tears, we shared every part,
you planted the seeds of resilience in my
heart.

When darkness lingered and shadows would
creep,
you offered your light, a promise to keep.
An angel in disguise, you lifted my gaze,
turning my struggles into vibrant displays.

With every lesson, you taught me to fly,
to reach for the stars, to dream and to try.
So here in this moment, my gratitude flows,
for all that you've given, more than you know.

Thank you for being my guiding embrace,
for showing me courage, for filling my space.
In the journey of life, I'll carry your grace,
for you are my angel, my heart's sacred place.

Vanishing Voices

In crowded aisles of glittering shelves,
where books stand proud, yet not themselves,
I search in vain for voices past,
for Indian classics, rich and vast.

No Hindi verse, no Urdu prose,
no tales in tongues our soil knows.
Dramatists, poets, storytellers grand,
now lost to time, like grains of sand..

The branded shelves hold shallow dreams,
pages dressed in empty themes.
Where once there bloomed a sacred art,
now lie bestsellers with hollow hearts.

I wander through rows, but all I find,
are shiny covers, empty minds.
For where is the soul, the wisdom deep,
that once in ink did vigil keep?

Can money buy the writer's pen,
or birth a verse that speaks again?
For now it seems, with wealth and fame,
any fool can play the writer's game.

The voices of old, silenced, gone,
left behind in a world withdrawn.
Our roots in ink, grow hard to trace,
lost to a taste we can't replace.

Oh, bring them back—the stories rare,
of language rich, of love and care.
For India's heart lies hidden still,
in books unread, on shelves left chill.

Screams of Revolution

They gathered, voices young and raw,
students in protest, hearts burning bright,
chanting for justice under night's gaze—
a fight for rights, a cry for light.

But soon came silence, fierce and cold,
as riotous winds tore through the streets.
Smoke and screams blurred the heavy air,
their voices drowned by marching feet.

Names forgotten, futures erased,
some arrested, some laid to rest—
and still, their dreams haunt the nights
that saw their courage put to the ultimate
test.

Power played its ruthless hand,
twisting truths with brutal ease;
words bent low, untruths unleashed,
while shadows crept like spreading disease.

An iron fist veiled in flags unfurled,
a government draped in fascist might—
and in that year's despairing whirl,
a nation watched, gripped tight by fright.

But somewhere in the silence deep,
the whispers of the fallen grow—
an echo we are sworn to keep,
a fire they planted, still aglow.

Eyes Turned Away

Smoke rises, thick with the scent of lives—
lives burned, voices silenced, drowned.
A whisper drifts to my ear,
heavy with grief, laden with pain.
"Who is it?" my mind questions,
"A man? A woman? A child?
A Jew or a Muslim? Palestinian or Israeli?"
"No," my heart replies. "It is a human."

My eyes fall on a woman,
clad in cloth torn and worn,
her face twisted in fear, fleeing a faceless
mob.
I look away.

I turn my gaze again and see—
a child, latched to his mother's cold breast,
unmoving, unknowing, clinging to silence.
I look away.

A woman stands in waiting, eyes fixed on the
horizon,
for her lover, her brother, her son—
but he lies buried beneath broken stone,
in a wasteland of ruins, never to return.
I look away.

A hand lies still, fingers splayed to the sky,
asking for mercy, or perhaps for justice,
but I stand here silent, unmoved,
my gaze drifting again.

For I am humankind, the silent witness,
turning my eyes from horrors untold,
a passive glance, a heart turned cold,
as lives are lost, as souls unfold.

And in each act of looking away,
I too am buried, day by day.

To Kafka, Across Time

I wish I could time travel,
To step through the veil and find you there,
Lost in the quiet of your mind,
Where every word feels like a prayer.
I'd walk the streets of Prague with you,
Your gaze as distant as the stars,
And say the things you never heard,
That you were loved, despite the scars.
I'd hug you, tight, and hold you near,
To whisper truths you never knew:
That life is worth the struggle, friend,
And you were always meant to bloom.
Your father's words, so cruel, so cold,
I'd shatter them with love's warm light,
I'd tell you, softly, "You are enough,
More than enough, with all your might."

I'd show you how the world will change,
How centuries will sing your name,
And though the darkness wraps you tight,
Your words would spark an endless flame.
For in your ink, the truth is clear,
That in our hearts, you'll always live,
And all your pain, your quiet fears,
Are what you gave, and we forgive.

Reunion

The years have passed, but here we stand,
A circle of smiles, a familiar band.
We've wandered roads both far and wide,
But still, our hearts beat side by side.
Laughter spills like summer rain,
The weight of time now feels like grain,
Soft and gentle, worn by days,
Yet still we find the same old ways.
The college halls may seem far gone,
But memories linger, they carry on.
Late-night talks, those coffee cups,
The dreams we held, the times we'd bluff.
We've lived, we've lost, we've learned, we've grown,
But in this room, we're all still home.

The years may change, but here we see
That we are still the "we" we used to be.
A toast to friendship, fierce and true,
To all the paths we each pursue.
But nothing, not a single thing,
Will change the joy these moments bring.
And when we part, and time moves on,
We'll know this bond will carry strong,
For college friends, like stars, remain,
Shining through every joy and pain.

In Search of a Quiet Café

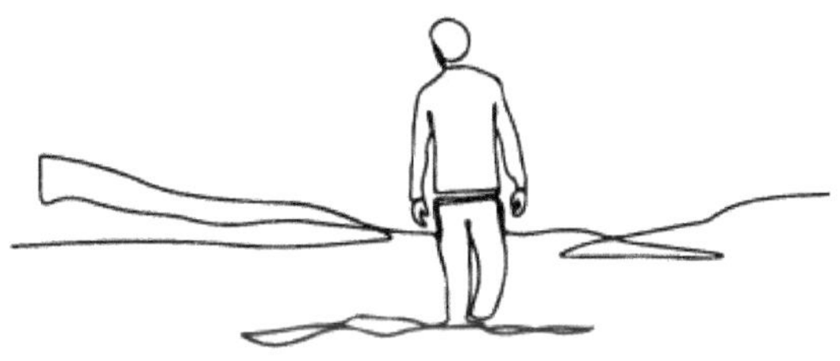

I wander through the streets of Doon,
Where silence once was soft, sweet tune—
A city draped in gentle ease,
Where time moved slowly like a whispered
breeze.
Not long ago, cafés were rare,
A foreign thought, beyond compare.
We'd roam just to pass the time,
And talk of dreams we'd never climb.
But now the streets are lined with glass,
And crowded chairs where moments pass.
The cafés bloom like flowers wild,
In places where peace once beguiled.
I search for quiet, a place to be,
On these graves of what once set me free.

A little space, a subtle grace,
A sliver of the past's embrace.
And after much hustle, I find one,
A café where the day's still spun.
The past remains, though dimmed and faint,
An echo of what used to paint.
I step inside and heads all turn,
A different world for me to learn.
Couples lost in their glowing screens,
Youngsters snapping what they've seen.
An old lady, a man alone,
Reminiscing days that have long flown.
I sit, and watch, and quietly sigh,
Wondering if I'm out of time.
The music hums a distant past,
Yet everything feels far too fast.
The air is thick with words unsaid,
While all around, lives are led—
But not in tune, not as they were,
Each one alone, despite the blur.
And so I sit, my heart laid bare,
For in this café, there's no care.
I found the crowd, I found the sound,
But peace, it seems, is not around.

The ghosts of quiet have all fled,
Replaced by noise and things unsaid.
And I realize, with heavy sigh,
The quiet cafés are gone, gone by.
Now here I sit, amidst the strife,
In search of peace, but not of life.

Clouds Between Us

I've been yearning for solitude,
A moment to sit with the quiet hum of
myself.
Today, I found it—
A café corner, a cup of warm coffee,
Its bittersweet notes fleeting across my
tongue.
And then, the breeze—soft, insistent—
Whispered your name through the stillness.
It pulled me back to the winter we first met,
A shaded evening where shadows stretched
long,
Over coffee and carrot cake.
You, with a smile that tangled the air,
Me, too naive to fathom
The labyrinth of your love.

Now, in these lonely interludes,
I trace the gaps we couldn't bridge.
We both bore the weight of losing each
other—
Your love, a tempest I couldn't anchor,
Mine, a quiet stream you didn't see.
By the time we learned the language of us,
The pages had already turned.
I remember the rain—
How it cloaked us in its tender embrace,
Every meeting, a symphony of skies.
Drenched and laughing,
It felt like the heavens rejoiced
In the symphony of our fleeting moments.
But now, I wonder—
Will the rain ever hold us again,
The way it once did?
Will the clouds find their way
To soften the ache that lingers?
Or have we scattered too far,
Two halves of a love
That couldn't find its whole?

Where the Flags Flutter

Today, I wandered alone once more,
Through the lanes of the town where my roots
entwine.
Was it the streets and their stories I sought,
Or something within—a part of me, lost,
Hidden in the folds of time?
The Old Mussoorie Road called me again,
To a Tibetan café, my haven of stillness.
Here, nostalgia wrapped me in its quiet
storm—
Memories of a child in Dehradun's embrace,
Wide-eyed at the beauty of fluttering flags.
Green, blue, yellow, white, red—
Their dance in the wind held me spellbound.
I marveled as they swayed over serene heights,
But their secret eluded my young heart.

Today, curiosity led me to ask a monk,
A keeper of wisdom, serene and kind.
"What do these flags mean?" I ventured,
And he unraveled their ancient truth:
White is the wind, ever-moving, unseen.
Blue is the sky, vast, eternal, serene.
Red is the fire, a force that renews.
Green is the water, life's flowing muse.
Yellow is the earth, grounding us all.
Together, they are the essence of life,
An ode to the elements that sustain our
world.
Their colors remind us to tread with care,
To honor, to love, to share.
As I sat there, cradling his words,
The valley felt more than just a home.
It was a mirror, a map, a guide—
To the gratitude I'd forgotten to find,
To the pieces of myself still waiting to align.

Life, Like Lemon Tea

As I finished my meal, a thought unfurled—
A friend's clever quip, a Gen Z word: *Hangry.*
At first, I stared, confused,
But curiosity nudged, and Google amused.
There it was—a mix of hunger and ire,
A Frankenstein word, born of playful desire.
I laughed, bemused, at my lagging pace,
But found solace in my love for language's
grace.
Sinking deep into the whirl of my musings,
I sipped on my post-meal ritual—tea brewing.
Honey, ginger, lemon— a soothing trinity,
Though too tart for my taste initially.
Sip by sip, it mellowed and bloomed,
A symphony of flavors, the sharpness
consumed.

And then it struck—a lesson so true,
Life is no different, it brews like tea too.
At first, it can be sour, hard to take,
A sharpness of trials, a lingering ache.
But give it time, let it steep in its way,
And you'll find it flows, smooth and okay.
Life doesn't come at you—it comes from
within,
A dance of resilience, a rhythm to begin.
Like tea, it teaches, one sip at a time,
To savor the moments, both tart and sublime.

What Makes a Day Good?

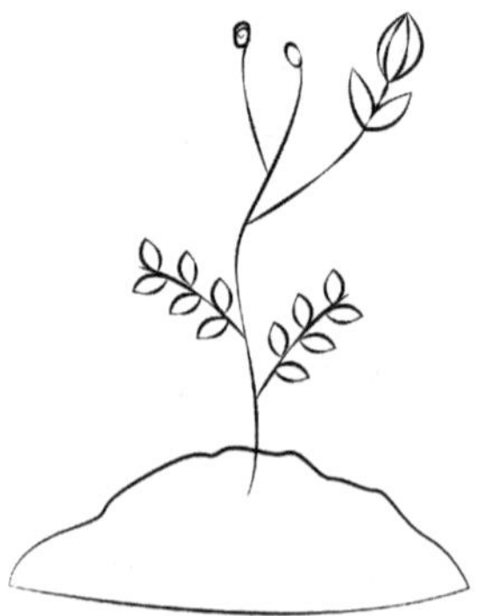

When does a day earn its worth?
Is it in tending to oneself,
In moments of care, where body and soul
align?
Or is it in scaling peaks of ambition,
Where applause meets the sound of one's
climb?
Is it counted in coins, in fame's fleeting glow,
A tally of triumphs the world can bestow?
Or perhaps it is nestled in the warmth of kin,
In shared laughter, where memories begin?

Could it lie in the grasp of an old friend's
hand,
In stories retold, in bonds that withstand?
Or is it a lie we tell to make peace,
With days that dissolve, with moments that
cease?
What makes a day "good,"
When the lines blur and meanings shift?
Is it the joy of the journey, the gift of breath,
Or is it the questions we carry, unanswered
yet?
Maybe no day is wholly good,
Nor wholly bad—it simply is.
A canvas we stain with colors we choose,
Each hue is a reflection of what we win or
lose.
Perhaps the answer lies not in the day,
But in the way we live, in what we embrace.
To call it well spent, to make it our own,
Is to find meaning in the mundane, the
known.

The Bliss of Togetherness

There is a quiet joy in their company,
In the soft laughter that fills the air,
A peace found only in the spaces shared,
Where love lingers, simple and rare.
When my mother speaks, her voice is home,
A gentle melody that calms my mind.
Her wisdom, like sunlight, warms my soul,
And in her presence, I feel aligned.
My father's laughter, deep and steady,
A foundation that steadies my heart.
In his eyes, there's a knowing, ready
To guide me, never too far apart.

The moments seem small, yet they are vast,
A shared meal, a quiet walk through the trees,

Time slows, and I realize at last,
This is bliss—just being at ease.
No grand gestures or fleeting things,
Just the comfort of being where love sings.
In their presence, I find my place,
In their warmth, I find my grace.
For the greatest gift, I've come to see
Is not what we do, but simply to be,
In the warmth of family, where hearts are
free,
A timeless bliss, forever with me.

The Bond That Remains

I flipped through pages, old photographs,
A journey through time, memories that last.
A picture of laughter, of days well-spent,
With my sisters, my second mothers,
heaven-sent.
There we were, nestled in simple joy,
Laughing, dancing, no care to destroy
The magic we held in the warmth of our
hearts,
From guavas to pomelos, we shared every
part.
We played games until the day turned to
night,
In the glow of our bond, everything felt right.
Our souls were entwined in a perfect dance,
The kind that only time could enhance.

Though the years have passed, and we've all grown,
The threads of togetherness are still sewn.
Through life's changes, the love remains,
A constant rhythm, despite the pains.
The time we shared was so pure, so divine,
are treasures we hold, forever mine.
My sisters, my second mothers, my guide,
In their love, I'll always confide.

Leaving Home

I pack my bags, the journey ahead,
Delhi awaits, but a heaviness treads.
It's only a few days, just a short while,
Yet each step away feels like miles.
The door closes behind me with a soft sound,
But inside, my heart lingers around.
A tug, a pull, a quiet ache,
The familiar comforts I'm about to forsake.
I feel the weight of goodbye unspoken,
Like threads of home are slowly broken.
Guilt settles in, though I don't know why,
As if leaving is a reason to cry.
The city calls, with its promise of change,
But my heart stays where memories arrange,
In the warmth of my parents' care,
In the place where love fills the air.

I miss them more than I can say,
Even though I'll be back one day.
It's not about distance or the time apart,
But the constant ache in my heart.
So I step into the unknown,
With bittersweet feelings of being alone.
But I know I'll return, and when I do,
The love of home will see me through.